Neomedievalism, Neoconservatism, and the War on Terror

Neomedievalism, Neoconservatism, and the War on Terror

Bruce Holsinger

PRICKLY PARADIGM PRESS
CHICAGO

Prickly Paradigm Press, LLC
5629 South University Avenue
Chicago, Il 60637

www.prickly-paradigm.com

ISBN: 0-9761475-9-9
ISBN-13: 978-0-9761475-9-6
LCCN: 2007929753

Printed in the United States of America on acid-free paper.

To the seeming surprise of some, our enemies have brains. They are constantly adapting and adjusting to what we're doing. They combine medieval sensibilities with modern technology and media savvy to find new ways to exploit perceived weaknesses and to weaken the civilized world.

—Secretary of Defense Donald Rumsfeld, *testifying before the Senate Appropriations Committee, April 25, 2005*

We cannot not periodize.

—Fredric Jameson, *A Singular Modernity* (2002)

Preface

"In the world of today, the worst fate that can befall a human being is to be stateless." So wrote the great Princeton historian Joseph Strayer at the opening of his classic study *On the Medieval Origins of the Modern State*. Published in 1970, though based on lectures and courses given over the preceding decade, Strayer's book discerned in certain premodern bureaucracies — Angevin, Norman, Burgundian — the seeds of modern statecraft, suggesting that the strict divide between the pre- and post-Westphalian worlds long cherished by European historians had been greatly exaggerated. During the period in which he was working out this deceptively straightforward thesis, Strayer, along with a hand-picked group of fellow Princeton faculty members, had also been serving the Central Intelligence Agency as an advisor to the Office of National Estimates, participating in regular meetings with CIA Director Allen W. Dulles. It has been speculated that the work of the so-called Princeton Consultants provided a crucial basis of intelligence for the illegal and brutally effective covert operations during this phase of the Cold War aimed at overthrowing governments in Brazil, the Dominican Republic, Chile, and elsewhere.

What, we might ask, could a medievalist have been doing for the CIA? As a historian of medieval diplomatic history, Strayer, it seems, was hired as someone who knew a bit about state formation: about the (often violent) processes of statecraft and bureaucracy-building necessary to ushering the messy amalgam of underdeveloped political formations into the modern pantheon of nation-states. As Strayer avowed, "Only the most remote and primitive peoples can do without the state."

Salim Ahmed Hamdan would likely agree with Strayer's assessment of the perils of statelessness. Hamdan was captured by American forces shortly after the start of the Afghanistan war in 2001; since then he has been detained at Guantánamo Bay along with hundreds of other prisoners taken during the conflict. *Hamdan v. Rumsfeld*, a case decided by the U.S. Supreme Court in June of 2006, served during the appeals process as a testing-ground of sorts for assertions of presidential authority in the face of established international law and the dictates of treaties regarding the American treatment of enemy combatants. Unlike the vast majority of detainees at Guantánamo who have not been charged with any crime or been shown to have any specific terrorist affiliation, Hamdan has openly admitted serving as a driver and bodyguard to Osama bin Laden from 1996 to 2001, training at an al Qaeda camp, and moving weapons among members of the organization.

Though a citizen of Yemen, however, and despite the Supreme Court's insistence on the illegality of the military commission apparatus invented to try him and other detainees, Hamdan remains — in the eyes of the law — stateless. As a member of al Qaeda, a transnational organization unmoored from the political and geographical coordinates of a particular nation, he exists as a "non-state actor," without the rights and privileges accorded to state citizens under international law. Non-state actors detained at Guantánamo and elsewhere are, of course, not regarded as prisoners of war, but as "enemy combatants," an ad hoc category that ideally embodies the bogus legalities that the Bush administration has substituted for reason and evidence. As has often been noted, when Texas governor George W. Bush proclaimed during the 2000 presidential campaign that his administration would spurn the idealistic project of "nation building," he was echoing the pragmatic, Scowcroftian realism that typified his father's administration, particularly in its conduct of the Gulf War. Since September 11, by contrast, Bush's counter-embrace of the neoconservatism of his new advisors has led to an enthusiastic era of nation building, or at least the rhetorical accoutrements thereof. In the process, neoconservatism has deliberately and cleverly left behind those whose nations and states remain *un*built, unable to inhabit the international sphere of state action and national belonging. A perilous statelessness now defines the legal identity of this Yemeni citizen — a statelessness that signals, as one justice put it in a concurrence handed down with the *Hamdan* decision at the Circuit Court level, the "non-eligible party's failure to be a nation."

It is in this failure that Salim Ahmed Hamdan is to be understood, by the relentless logic of neoconservative historicism, as *medieval man*. Like his cohorts and comrades in al Qaeda and the Taliban, he is not to be named and understood as "medieval" simply for his barbarism, his backwardness, his allegiance to a ruthlessly violent conjunction of theological fundamentalism and mass murder. Rather, as we shall see, his role as unruly medieval subject in a modern world derives from what the neoconservatives are beginning to recognize as the strategic and tactical opportunities afforded by a collective "failure to be modern" shared by friend and foe alike. Medieval man is to be feared, imprisoned, and, most importantly of all, learned from, precisely for his perceived ability to render irrelevant the authority, territorial integrity, and jurisdictions of modern nations — nations that are the raison d'être of the neoconservative worldview. In the world of today, to modify Strayer's dictum, one of the worst fates that can befall a human being is to be rendered medieval.

The critique of neoconservatism inspiring this project has two closely related aims — the first largely polemical, the second more narrowly analytical — that correspond to the two parts of the book. Part I provides a critical overview of what I am calling the 9/11 premodern: the varieties and modes of medievalist and medievalizing discourse in the wake of the 2001 attacks. Far from an unfortunate cliché, as John Burns and others would have it, post-9/11 medievalism became a dominant journalistic and political paradigm for comprehending the identity, culture, and motivations of America's perceived enemy during the first few years of the War on Terror. Both an endless source of conveniently simplified propaganda and a weird kind of historical autism, the 9/11 premodern continues to function as a reservoir of descriptive fallacy and misrecognition in America's prosecution of global war.

Accordingly, the second part of the book turns from the cloying rhetoric of post-9/11 medievalism to the more particular domain of *neomedievalism*, a fairly recent school of thought in current International Relations theory whose emergence is closely tied to the rise of non-state global actors — NGOs, transnational corporations, organizations like al Qaeda, corporate militias, and so on — as dominant forces in the international political sphere. An analytically powerful and increasingly influential mode of understanding the post-9/11 world and of acting within its currents, neomedievalism has interesting (if invariably abnegated) ties to modernization theory, particularly in its creative understanding of the Middle Ages and its political formations as complex engines of modernity.

Yet despite its realist academic respectability, neomedievalism — and this will be the underlying argument of what follows — has begun to play a much more insidious role in the War on Terror than its more conventional counterpart. In many ways the seemingly banal and ubiquitous language of medievalism has served as an ideological distraction from the quite specific operations of *neo*medievalism on the levels of policy planning and legal argument in the Bush administration. The brief test cases for this assertion will be the language of force restructuring at Donald Rumsfeld's Pentagon and, ultimately, the so-called Torture Memos, positioned here as the culminating exemplification of what I see as the historical learning process undergone by neoconservatism since September 11. Both examples provoke a strong degree of pessimism at the much-touted notion of the 2006 elections as a death-knell of sorts for neoconservatism (as does the equally touted "surge" announced by the president in January of 2007, a policy scripted by neoconservatives at the American Enterprise Institute). Neoconservatism, *mutatis mutandis*, is here to stay, and the closer we examine its language and logic, the more solid will be the grounds for resisting the historical ideology it seeks to naturalize as global political inevitability. If we inhabit a New Middle Ages, as the neomedievalists would have us believe, the neoconservatives would convince us that even this epoch of porous borders, scattered hegemonies, and transnational technologies must yield, however reluctantly, to America's engines of democratizing idealism.

PART I:
The 9/11 Premodern

Arguably over the last several years, no single person on this planet has had the blood of more innocent men, women and children on his hands than Zarqawi. He personified the dark, sadistic, and medieval vision of the future-of beheadings, suicide bombings, and indiscriminate killings.

—Secretary of Defense Donald Rumsfeld,
on the death of Abu Musab al-Zarqawi
(June 7, 2006)

Barbaric Irruptions

On September 14, 2001, Thomas Friedman devoted his column in *The New York Times* to what he termed the "civil war within Islam," an epochal struggle pitting the modernizing advocates of progressive democratization across the Near and Middle East against the reactionary forces of Islamist fundamental-ism. As Friedman described it, this civil war symbolized a larger reordering of world alliances equal in its impact to the momentous geopolitical upheavals of the twen-tieth century. "Just as World Wars I and II produced new orders and divisions," Friedman wrote, "so too might this war." One such division stretches across a chasm not of place, belief, or population, however, but of time. The global struggle made visible on September

11 must be understood not simply in terms of a political conflict between moderation and fanaticism,
Friedman contended, but as a battle for the very
historical soul of Islam — a battle waged across the
region "between the modernists and the medievalists."
Here, just three days after the attacks, in the nation's
newspaper of record and in the words of its most
respected columnist, Osama bin Laden had become a
"medievalist."

What a curious choice of words, I thought at
the time; and as Friedman's pronouncement quickly
became an organizing metaphor for that pervasive
metonymy known as the "War on Terror," the single
term "medievalist" continued to nag at my apprehen-
sion of September 11 and its aftermath. That my own
professional identity coincided precisely with
Friedman's designation for bin Laden became the
starting point for an investigation that has led me in a
direction I did not expect: an investigation in which my
own academic expertise has more often than not
seemed frustratingly beside the point. This frustration,
in fact, has remained central to my thinking about all
that follows here. In standard academic parlance, a
medievalist is a scholar of the history and civilization of
what we commonly call the Middle Ages, a period
stretching roughly from the fifth century of the
Common Era through the fifteenth: an era that
embraces the final fall of the Roman Empire, the rise
and triumph of Islam, and the Crusades fought over
Jerusalem and the Holy Land; a millennium that gave
us Mohammed, Charlemagne, the Koran, the Book of
Kells, courtly love, Ghengis Khan, feudalism, the Jin

dynasty, Hildegard of Bingen, St. Francis of Assisi, Dante, Marco Polo, Petrarch, Chaucer, the Aztec empire, the cathedral of Notre Dame, and the English kings Shakespeare would immortalize in plays such as *Richard III* and *Henry V*. We medievalists study and teach the life and culture of this vast expanse of history, whether Eastern or Western, usually specializing in a particular period or region of medieval culture from the perspective of a certain academic discipline. A medievalist working in an art history department, for example, might have made a career studying stained glass windows in French cathedrals and parish churches, while a medievalist employed in Asian Studies may be an expert on the literature of thirteenth-century Japan. Beyond the academy, *medievalism* can describe anything from the mock swordfights of the Society for Creative Anachronism and the Brother Cadfael mysteries of Ellis Peters to the popularized retelling of Templar history in *The Da Vinci Code* and the neo-Gothic design of Our Lady of Walsingham Catholic Church in Houston, Texas. University medievalists — that is, those paid by an institution of higher education to profess a specialty in the historical Middle Ages themselves — thus inhabit a relatively narrow band along the spectrum of American medievalisms today.

To blithely describe Osama bin Laden and his ilk as "medievalists," then, is to impute a host of complex and often contradictory associations to the perpetrators of a particular criminal act of mass murder. At the same time, however, it speaks to the concerted effort among the nation's political class in the two years following the September 11 attacks to engage al Qaeda and its Taliban supporters in a war over temporality: to embody their avowed antiwesternism as antimodernism. It was on the sixteenth day of the same month that President George W. Bush made his infamous remark during a hastily assembled news conference on the South Lawn of the White House: "This crusade, this war on terrorism, is going to take a while." The next day, on the floor of the House of Representatives, Congressman Dana Rohrabacher (R-CA) chimed in by asserting that "The Taliban were and are medieval in their words, in their world view, and their religious view. They are violent, they are intolerant, they are fanatics that are totally out of sync with Muslims throughout the world." The very long and mind-numbingly repetitive list goes on, and its implications seem in retrospect frighteningly clear. This "clash of civilizations," in Samuel P. Huntington's much-invoked phrase, had suddenly become a clash of millennia.

As these examples begin to suggest, the questions raised by post-9/11 medievalism are legion. Why decry al Qaeda's supposed "medievalism" rather than its patently transnational modernity? Why invoke the Crusades as the historical analogy for this new global struggle rather than, say, the Cold War? Why, in other words, go back to the twelfth century when the twentieth furnishes such a hauntingly recent array of precedents?

There are some readily available answers to such questions. Imagining the September 11 attacks as acts of "medievalism" divides the world along an axis simultaneously of history and geography, placing the West on the side of modernity and Islamism on the side of the primitive, the archaic, the premodern. Such a political logic of periodization inspires Timothy Lynch, the director of the Project on Criminal Justice at the libertarian Cato Institute, in his testimony before the Senate Judiciary Committee's Subcommittee on Administrative Oversight and the Courts. Lynch's purpose in his December 2001 appearance was to register objections to a series of judicial procedures instigated by the Bush administration to handle accused war criminals apprehended on U.S. soil and abroad: the suspension of due process, the issuance of executive arrest warrants in defiance of the Fourth Amendment's provisions against unreasonable search and seizure, and other similar procedures aimed at "streamlining" the prosecutions of those the administration deemed "enemy combatants." What distinguished Lynch's testimony from that of many of his political counterparts was its forthright objections to the abrogations of the human rights of detainees who had been shipped to Guantánamo and elsewhere. As one of the few conservative critics of the Bush administration's rush to war in the months following the September attacks, Lynch took his extended exchange with the Senate subcommittee as an opportunity to criticize the executive branch's preemptively ad hoc approach to the legality of detainment, warning of its dire consequences in the event of possible further domestic attacks. In the prepared statement that opened his testimony, however, Lynch sought to appeal to the subcommittee's deeply engrained sense of

American exceptionalism in drawing a sharp historical dividing line between the 9/11 hijackers and the nation they attacked:

> The horrific attacks of September 11th have made it painfully clear that a technologically sophisticated band of medieval barbarians have declared war on America. In my view, these barbarians hold a nihilist philosophy and have nothing but contempt for human life. They attacked America because our nation is seen as a symbol of respect for individual rights. America is a unique nation in all of world history because it is founded upon a Constitution that is designed to acknowledge and enhance the importance and dignity of human beings.
>
> We must respond to this new threat without losing sight of what we are fighting for. Our troops are not simply defending the property and occupants of some geographical location. They are defending the fundamental American idea that individuals have the right to life, liberty, and the pursuit of happiness. Our government must fight any foreign or domestic enemy who would destroy the rights of our people.

The almost willful oxymoron that opens Lynch's prepared statement — "a technologically sophisticated band of medieval barbarians" — cannot obscure the historical lesson his testimony seems designed to teach: that the perpetrators of the 9/11 attacks are separated from their symbolic national target not primarily by religion or region, but, again, by time. Lynch's positioning of the attacks within the impossibly broad embrace of "all of world history" registers a key and recurring element of post-9/11 medievalism. The terrorists do not act medieval, they *are* medieval, their putative role as "barbarians" standing in violent and "nihilist" opposition to the Constitution of the United States. If the attacks can be imagined as an assault not simply on America but on its founding document, the Constitution, then the September 11 hijackers have undermined the very political embodiment of Enlightenment rationalism. One of the great registers of political modernity, American constitutionalism is also the *sine qua non* of the nation's victory over a benighted prenational past.

Lynch's opening statement reads in hindsight more like an emotional grasp for an abjecting metaphor than an attempt at serious analysis. Nevertheless, though the Bush administration would disavow the similarly medieval resonances of the president's "crusade," September 11 immediately began to function as a kind of medievalizing engine in American political discourse, churning out an array of historical dualisms separating a modern West from a premodern world that had finally responded to the long arm of modernity with a morning of cataclysmic violence. Post-9/11 medievalism functions, too, as a means of reducing a host of very complex geopolitical forces to a simple historical equation, freeing its users from the demands of subtlety, nuance, and a rigorous historical understanding of the nature of inter- and supra-national conflict in an era of globalization. In this temporal bisecting of the world, America's enemies inhabit an unchanging medieval space equivalent in many ways to the monolithic East imagined in

Orientalist discourses of the eighteenth and nineteenth centuries. One of the more obvious rhetorical effects of 9/11, in fact, has been to reenergize the enduring interplay of medievalism and Orientalism.

Another explanation is related but more purely rhetorical. While medievalism shares with terrorism a resistance to clear or easy definition, the connotative intimacy of the two terms explains in part the ubiquity of post-9/11 medievalism. Consider, for example, this discussion of the word *terrorism* offered in Jonathan Barker's widely read *No-Nonsense Guide to Terrorism*, a useful recent guide to the international climate after September 11:

> Recognizing the emotional force of the topic, experts often try to burnish feelings of righteous-ness rather than strive to enlighten understanding and challenge prejudice. They use the words "terrorism" and "terrorist" to denote the actions, ideas, people and organizations that, from their standpoint, lie beyond the boundaries of reason, ethics and interest that govern ordinary poli-tics...Without a clear and pertinent definition the words "terrorist" and "terrorism" are counters in propaganda wars that obscure analysis of the fright-ful acts they are often used to describe.

According to this critical account, terrorism operates as a lexical contrivance that affords those who wield it a historical alibi for prejudice, righteousness, and obscu-rantism. *Terrorist* functions both as a sign of irrational-ity and moral negation, in other words, and as a trope resorted to in order to resist clear analysis of particular forms of violence. It would not be much of a stretch, however, to substitute the words "medievalist" for Barker's "terrorist" and "medievalism" for "terrorism." Before September 11, this substitution would not have made much sense to the general reader. Post-9/11, though, it perfectly accords with the ubiquitous presence of medievalism in contemporary discussions of terrorism, suggesting the common tendency of the two terms to evoke a particular mentality, behavior, or worldview.

Such observations, however, afford a series of necessary starting points rather than any kind of analytical specificity, and I invoke them here only to register the powerful role that the Middle Ages have played in channeling the historical current of political rhetoric following the events of 2001. For history, of course, is no more conducive to clarity of thought in our current political climate than terrorism itself. Post-9/11 medievalism embodies in a particularly spectacular way the grave distortions of the near and distant past involved in the War on Terror: by al Qaeda under the banner of religious purity; by the United States government under the sign of neoimperial right; and the list goes on.

Yet a firm commitment to history is hardly an unambiguously democratic (let alone progressive) ideal. If we like to lambaste our nation's leaders for their failure to learn from the past, we should also recognize that similar failures have virtually defined the rhetoric of violent engagement informing various conflicts in the Middle East over the last quarter century. The authors of the Charter of Hamas (1988), for instance, possessed a very strong sense of history, invoking the medieval Crusades nearly a dozen times while imputing the modern world's most tumultuous conflicts to the machinations of a Jewish conspiracy: the "Zionist interests" that inspired the French Revolution, fomented the Communist revolution in Russia, started World War I "so as to wipe out the Islamic Caliphate," "established the League of Nations in order to rule the world," and "stood behind World War II, where they collected immense benefits from trading with war materials." A vastly more perverse abuse of history than Bush's thoughtless invocation of "crusade," this twisted vision of the course of modern events stresses an aspect of historical rhetoric that is as obvious as it is worth repeating: that the "voice of history," in Gibbon's words from *The Decline and Fall of the Roman Empire*, often functions as "little more than the organ of hatred or flattery."

As is the case with many catastrophes of global implications, the subtler tones of history's voice were muted by September 11. Those of us who make it our life's work to study the history of the millennium our cultural traditions have dubbed the Middle Ages and teach its civilization to American students have watched in despair over the last several years at the reduction of the medieval to the level of glib and unconsidered analogy (leading NYU's Carolyn Dinshaw, with tongue in cheek, to propose the founding of a post-9/11 organization called Concerned Medievalists for Peace). In the face of this rhetorical enlistment of the Middle Ages, professional medievalists have responded by organizing panels, speaking at conferences, and writing critical articles addressing the

widespread misappropriations of their period in the
service of the War on Terror. Most have chosen a
corrective response, publishing responsible and
complex accounts of the Crusades, resisting popularized homogenizations of history by recording the
diverse course of East-West relations, and emphasizing
important distinctions within Islam and Christianity in
their various historical incarnations. One of the schol-
ars I admire most in my own field told me that one of
her responses to the American war on the Taliban was
to start reading as much as she could about medieval
Afghanistan — a period in which the Ghaznavid
dynasty created an Islamic empire far greater in its artistic imagination and cultural dynamism than any
contemporaneous European kingdom. And at least one
blog by an academic medievalist devotes itself to expos-
ing and correcting bogus appropriations of the Middle
Ages in the media, political discourse, and popular
culture (taking on Nicholas D. Kristoff for "going out
of his way to bitch-slap the middle ages for no good
reason" in a column on Iran's treatment of journalists).
Such informed ripostes from medievalists in the academy are of course invaluable tools for intervention in
this wilfully antihistorical milieu, and there are any
number of popularized misconceptions about the
Middle Ages that are very much worth correcting.

It seems to me, though, that this vulgarly
medievalizing habit of mind is now too deeply
entrenched within the political class's basic comprehension of the implications and meaning of September
11 to offer any hope of factual correction. Our urge to
set the historical record straight (an urge I share, and

one to which I give in more than once in what follows) must go hand in hand with an honest admission that the War on Terror has transmogrified the medieval into something well beyond the grasp of our expertise and, in many cases, even our comprehension. To suggest, therefore, that medievalists have some kind of special obligation to address (let alone a privileged vantage-point from which to address) the recruitment of the Middle Ages in this rhetorical milieu is to fall into the same medievalizing trap set by Friedman, Bush, and numerous others.

For medievalism in this climate has become the historical handmaiden of a renewed anti-intellectualism that casts suspicion on any politically-minded utterance from within the American university as the sign of a debased leftism that flirts with outright treason. Particularly vulnerable to this line of attack have been professors in the squishier humanities disciplines, whose supposed intellectual justifications for terrorism were repeatedly uncovered in the months after September 11. Thus Jonah Goldberg, in a widely-read column for *The National Review* published that November, responds to allegations of al Qaeda's primitivism with an image of the group's leader as the product of pernicious literary criticism: "Osama bin Laden — with his satellite phones, his Postcolonial Studies Cliff Notes, and his hunger for nuclear weapons — is not a creature from the past, he is a creature of today." Ward Churchill, a professor of Ethnic Studies at the University of Colorado (my own former institution), posts an Internet essay on the day of the attacks that goes virtually unread for the next three years yet, when "discovered" by College Republicans in upstate New York, inspires serious national discussions about whether the death penalty might be justified for what the governor of Colorado himself identified as Churchill's "treasonous statements." And the American Council of Trustees and Alumni, an organization founded by Lynne Cheney and Senator Joseph Lieberman, among others, issues a report titled *Defending Civilization: How Our Universities Are Failing America and What Can Be Done About It*, which includes a long appendix listing by name over one hundred students and faculty cited for "blaming America" for the September 11 attacks. "When a nation's intellectuals are unwilling to defend its civilization," the report avows, "they give comfort to its adversaries."

We might turn for consolation to Plato's *Gorgias*, one of the great critiques of the rhetoric of anti-intellectualism in the Western tradition. In the words of Socrates to Gorgias, a professional rhetor, "the rhetorician need not know the truth about things; he has only to discover some way of persuading the people that he has more knowledge than those who know." There could be no better way to describe the rhetorical engines of medievalism as they have functioned since September 11. The effect has been a mass enlistment of all things medieval into a global conflict in which the Middle Ages function as a reservoir of unconsidered analogy and reductive propaganda. This language seems perfectly designed in this respect to take advantage of America's professed historical ignorance by capitalizing on an ideological monopoly of germane knowledge. In the case of the Middle Ages, "the truth about things," in Socrates's words, has been rendered all but irrelevant, and the dominant political discourse has established an empty historical palaver in its place.

Yet who could possibly disagree with the urgent defense of history articulated by Lynne Cheney on October 5, 2001? "At a time of national crisis," she enjoined on that day, "we need to encourage the study of our past.... We need to know, in a war, exactly what is at stake." Moments of "national crisis," however, are precisely those moments in which the past shows itself most vulnerable to manipulation, particularly during a war whose American prosecutors have made an attempt at a kind of ersatz intellectual buttressing by arguing for the exemplarity of the various historical pasts they have selected as most conducive to their policies. To enlist Cheney's own words, we need to know, in a war, exactly what is at stake in our leaders' insistent misuse of the language of history.

A Recurring War?

It was Clio herself, in fact, who was responsible for providing one of the few moments of comic relief in the months following the attacks. I refer here to the widely promoted "history lesson" that George W. Bush started receiving at the initiation of his political advisors in the months following September 11. One of the books recommended to Bush in the attacks' immediate aftermath was James Reston's *Warriors of God*, a popularized history of the Third Crusade that focuses on the personalities of its avowedly chivalrous and noble antagonists, Richard the Lionheart and Saladin, and that was published earlier in 2001. According to Karl Rove, the President "was sort of dismissive in the beginning of the Saladin book. But then he got into it and told me he enjoyed it." This putative enjoyment on Bush's part works to instill admiration for a chief executive willing to learn from the past, and medievalists will surely be flattered to know that the period they claim as their own object of scrutiny has made its studied presence felt at the highest echelons of American power. Even while prosecuting a war against the Taliban and al Qaeda in Afghanistan and elsewhere, the American president reads diligently in ostensibly true and accurate accounts of the medieval past as a way to help understand and reiterate as part of international policy the enemy's investment in distorting this past so violently.

The book itself, then, becomes a unique test case for Bush administration, representing — as far as we know — the single published source from which Bush could have derived knowledge of the historical resonances of his ostensibly medievalizing rhetoric of crusade. What the media failed to report on was the sheer enormity of the errors of fact, omission, and construal characterizing Reston's *Warriors of God*, a book that proved by far the most widely cited account of this supposed medieval backdrop to September 11. Throughout the book, propagandizing chronicles are uncritically presented as straightforward historical documentation, mistranslations of Latin appear in numerous geographical and biographical descriptions, and so on. And if we take Karl Rove at his word — a big if, of course, for it implies that Bush would actually have read the books recommended to him — in *Warriors of God*, the president would necessarily have come across the author's description of Richard the Lionheart, in a simply breathtaking phrase, as "the greatest warrior and Arab-slayer on earth." This description of the medieval English king commits a solecism that nevertheless makes the book perfectly appropriate reading for the leader of this (abnegated) Western crusade: for of course, as one reviewer noted, the Europeans' "opponents" during the Third Crusade were mostly Turks, Kurds, Mamluks, and Ashkenazic Jews — "Arab-slayer" functions for Reston as a conveniently amalgamating sobriquet that conflates the Christians' opponents and victims into a single entity and erases central parts of the medieval history it pretends to examine responsibly.

Again, though, this abuse of history becomes interesting less for its obvious fallacies than for its immediate rhetorical absorption into the war on terror. Here we must reckon with one of many instances of Osama bin Laden's prescience in regard to the Bush administration's rhetoric of historical comprehension. Just two months earlier, in an October interview aired on Al Jazeera, bin Laden had warned,

> This is a recurring war. The original crusade brought Richard [the Lionheart] from Britain, Louis from France, and Barbarus from Germany. Today the crusading countries rushed as soon as Bush raised the cross. They accepted the rule of the cross.

Like Slobodan Milosevic (who repeatedly recalled the Serbs' medieval defeat by the Ottoman Turks to stir nationalist sentiment against Bosnian and Kosovar Muslims) and Saddam Hussein (who issued a postage stamp with portraits of himself and Saladin standing side by side), bin Laden has always loved this kind of

stirring premodern imagery. His public pronouncements and *fatwahs* from the mid-1990s onward have
constantly exploited the rhetorical and historical capital
of the Crusades in a string of symbolic medievalisms
that are simultaneously apocalyptic and tactical:

> The Arabian Peninsula has never — since God made
> it flat, created its desert, and encircled it with seas —
> been stormed by any forces like the crusader armies
> now spreading in it like locusts, consuming its riches
> and destroying its plantations.

> We are following with utmost concern the
> Crusaders' preparations to occupy the former capi-
> tal of Islam (Baghdad), loot the fortunes of the
> Muslims and install a puppet regime on you that
> follows its masters in Washington and Tel Aviv.

> We have recognised that one of the best, effective,
> and available means to devoid the aerial force of the
> crusading enemy of its content is by digging large
> numbers of trenches and camouflaging them in
> huge numbers.

The October 2001 interview, however, brought this
iconography to brilliantly absurd heights. It may well
be that Reston's book was given a space on the president's historical reading list as a direct result of this
interview, which finds bin Laden tactically manipulat-
ing the multinational iconography of the Crusades. If
the Third Crusade led by Richard of England, Louis of
France, and Frederick Barbarossa of Germany united
disparate kingdoms and empires under the cross of
Christian orthodoxy, bin Laden's image of Bush

"rais[ing] the cross" and the American allies' unquestioningly "accept[ing] the rule of the cross" transforms the original pre- or paranational medieval collectivity that launched the Crusades into the postnational formation of NATO. In bin Laden's implied formulation, Bush now raises the cross just as Clement III did in 1189; the United States assumes the mantle of global illegitimacy embodied in the medieval papacy; and America's European allies, rather than joining the new crusade in the spirit of voluntary servitude in which the medieval crusaders like to cloak themselves, kowtow to the American president's imperialist whims.

• • • •

Perhaps the voice in the mainstream media arguing most eloquently against the rush to war after September 11 was that of James Carroll, the *Boston Globe* columnist who won a National Book Award for his memoir of the Vietnam years, *American Requiem* (1997). Carroll's subsequent book, *Constantine's Sword* (2002), sketched a panoramic view of Jewish-Christian relations since late antiquity, taking in the Crusades, the Inquisition, and the history of modern Catholicism before and after the Second Vatican Council. Carroll was thus one of the few prominent American journalists who had previously reflected in great depth on the epoch that became such a rhetorical battleground in the wake of September 11. In a column written two weeks after the attacks, Carroll's life-long reflections on Western Christianity's historical burdens formed part of his visceral reaction ("vertigo," as he later described it) to Bush's invocation of crusade. "[F]ar from being a long-ago history that we can blithely abjure," Carroll avowed here, "the Crusades created a state of consciousness that still shapes the mind of the West." Nor is this medieval "state of consciousness" a kneejerk reaction to the violence of September 11; rather, it represents one of the "pillars of the Western mind that the Crusades put in place." When Carroll collected his post-9/11 columns for a 2004 book, he named it *Crusade: Chronicles of an Unjust War*, a title that centralized an image of militant religiosity as the direct medieval legacy to the War on Terror:

> If the American president was the person carrying the main burden of shaping a response to the catastrophe of September 11, his predecessor in such a grave role, nearly a thousand years earlier, was the Catholic pope.

Carroll's medievalism thus goes far beyond the rhetorical. What he proposes, in fact, is a nearly unmediated historical relationship between the crusading armies of twelfth-century Europe and the twenty-first-century War on Terror. As he put it in the 2001 editorial,

> The only way "this crusade, this war on terrorism," in the president's phrase, will not be a replay of past crimes and tragedies is if we repudiate not just the word crusade but the mind of the crusader.

It may seem churlish to assent to the political spirit of this impassioned plea while objecting to its letter. In many ways, however, Carroll's insistence that the United States conceived its War on Terror with "the mind of the crusader" is, at root, no more historically acute — and no less misleading — than the widespread objectification of al Qaeda, bin Laden, and the Taliban as "medieval." The two metaphors operate according to the same historical logic, the same confident essentialism, and they exhibit the same blindness to the rootedness of the American response to the violent emergence of political Islam in latter-day international conflict. To understand the mindset that inspired the War on Terror as the legacy of a dualistic clarity of thought inherited from the Middle Ages is willfully to misrecognize the origins of this same mindset in the muddy complexities of the modern world — a misrecognition, again, shared by radical left and religious right alike. Ward Churchill's appalling essay, "Some People Push Back: On the Justice of Roosting Chickens," which gained notoriety for its metaphorical depiction of victims in the World Trade Center as "little Eichmanns," includes an equally specious image of the 9/11 attackers taking up the legacy of their medieval brethren:

> The war in which they were combatants has been waged more-or-less continuously by the "Christian West" — now proudly emblematized by the United States — against the "Islamic East" since the time of the First Crusade, about 1000 years ago.

Like Carroll, bin Laden, and Bush himself, Churchill crams a millennium of complex historical relations and antagonisms into a small box of stale medievalism.

Follow the Money

Even those attempting to do a responsible job confronting the complexities of the attackers' methods and motives can be led astray by the intellectually doping effects of their own medievalism, which often functions as a kind of involuntary epistemological reflex. A prime example here is the American approach to the attackers' transnational financing mechanisms. As a number of inquiries into al Qaeda's money moving confirmed, one of the organization's primary strategies for shuttling its funds around the world both before and after 9/11 involved the system of *hawala*, which relies not on wire transfers and other recorded transactions, but rather on in-person cash deposits that reach their intended recipients through untraceable faxes, e-mails, and cell phones that are then shredded, deleted, or discarded. It has been estimated that countries such as Pakistan move and bank vastly more amounts of money via *hawala* than through regulated financial institutions, and according to an Interpol report published in 2000, the system exploits a "nearly infinite number of variations" in its contemporary usage.

The coverage of *hawala* after the 2001 attacks focused on its untraceability, but also emphasized its archaism and its endurance as a money-moving system in the non-Western world; as an October 3, 2001 article in *The New York Times* put it,

> The system was in place long before Western banking. The ancient Chinese used a similar method called "flying money," or *fei qian*. Arab traders used it as a means of avoiding robbery along the Silk Road.

The article goes on to paint a rustic portrait of agents in numerous countries, including the United States, engaging in daily illegal financial transactions totalling billions of dollars a year, all of which goes untaxed, untraced, and unaccounted for by those outside the system:

> Mr. Khan and his associate, found sitting cross-legged on the floor of their sparse office and sipping tea, keep transactions in a brown notebook on Mr. Khan's desk. When he receives a telephone call or a fax to confirm that money has been picked

up elsewhere in the world, the relevant page is torn out of the notebook. Even the new scrutiny prompted by the terror attacks on Sept. 11 is highly unlikely to disclose all the details of how Mr. bin Laden's money moves through the ancient system.

The *hawala* brokers sip tea, sit on floors, and scribble on paper, with only the incidental conveniences of a fax machine and a phone to suggest they aren't living in the fifteenth century.

At a House Financial Services Committee hearing in October 2001 on the subject of terrorist financial networks and proposals for their disruption, Representative Sue Kelly (R-NY) cited this *Times* piece to initiate a line of questioning concerning the mechanism of *hawala*, entering the article into the Congressional Record for that day's testimony. Kelly's interlocutors in the hearing were Jimmy Gurule, treasury undersecretary for enforcement, and Dennis Lormel, chief of the financial crimes section of the Criminal Investigations Division at the FBI, both of whom were presenting expert testimony to the subcommittee that day:

> KELLY: It [*The New York Times* article] talks about the bin Laden network, and it refers to a money exchange called hawala. Hawala is something that bothers me a great deal, because I don't see how — given the nature of the beast, how you're going to be able to address that with regard to drying up any money that's being moved. How would you combat this? And I'm throwing this out to each of you... And could we start with you, Mr. Lormel?

LORMEL: Yes, ma'am. I'm not familiar with the article, number one. I'll just speak from an investigative...

KELLY: Well, are you familiar with hawala?

LORMEL: Yes.

KELLY: Have you any idea about what we can do to try to stop or reach into that to regulate it?

LORMEL: In terms of regulation, no, ma'am, I would defer to the Department of Justice. But in terms of investigation, certainly we will do everything in terms of tracking back and exploiting all of our databases and exploiting the expertise of our fellow agencies in terms of tracking it back.

KELLY: Mr. Gurule?

GURULE: Yes, hawala, as you stated, and accurately so, it certainly complicates the ability to follow the money because, based upon a hawala system, money can be exchanged without the money ever being transferred from a foreign country into the United States.

KELLY: And therefore you have no record anywhere and you can't go to a database and try to extract it.

Lormel seems entirely ignorant of *hawala*, and his instant bureaucratic reaction to Kelly's question is to invoke the FBI's trusty "databases" — as if these databases could have any hope of capturing relevant data concerning the monies moving through this system. The official from Treasury, by contrast, grasps the system's impenetrability to American and European enforcement protocols. There is no way to "follow the money," Gurule informs the committee, leading Kelly to point out that *hawala* leaves "no record anywhere" that might be captured in Lormel's databases. In short, as any of its thousands of worldwide brokers could have informed the congressional subcommittee, *hawala* represents an ideal means of transferring money without oversight, whether for the purpose of financing Islamist militants or for sending American dollars from Chicago home to Jakarta. What is glaringly apparent, in other words, is the strategic suitability of adopting *hawala* as a favored method of eluding the kind of computerized data collecting on which American and European financial detection depends.

As the hearing progresses, however, the self-evident tactical resourcefulness of *hawala* in relation to American and European investigative jurisdictions is called increasingly into question. Here is Representative Caroline B. Maloney (D-NY) pressing the committee's two witnesses on the historical roots and implications of this financing network:

> MALONEY: I have always been of the opinion that the country needs stricter money laundering laws and enforcement, whether it's terrorism or the drug war. Cutting off the money that funds criminal activities is sometimes the most effective way for the government to stop unlawful acts. I would

like to know if you have any proof if hawala was involved in the September 11 attack — that medieval financing system? Do you have any indication that that was involved?

LORMEL: No, ma'am, not at this juncture. Certainly there are a lot of questionable cash transactions that we're looking at, and questionable cash that we're looking at. But at this point, we have no direct correlation.

MALONEY: But it seems from listening to your testimony today, we're talking about all types of high-tech sharing of information, sort of Star Wars technology. But what we're really looking at is a Middle-Age financing system that seems the prevalent way that they're moving their monies. The bank — the Al-Shameel Bank has correspondent accounts with European and other non-U.S. banks. What steps has the administration taken to identify these banks, and what steps have you taken to prevent money from Al-Shameel Bank from entering the U.S. banking system?

GURULE: Well, the Foreign Terrorist Asset Tracking Center is the vehicle that's being used to identify monies, bank accounts that are linked or associated with terrorists and terrorist organizations. And more specifically, we are taking advantage of and examining all relevant sources of intelligence: law enforcement intelligence, CIA intelligence and information, classified information, Bank Secrecy Act information, as well as open source public records information. So we're looking at a multiple array of different sources to make those determinations. We're doing it now.

Congresswoman Maloney's juxtaposition of "Star Wars technology" and "a Middle-Age financing system" perfectly illustrates the principle of misrecognition I'm talking about here. On the one hand, organizations like al Qaeda are daily enlisting mechanisms such as *hawala* — "that medieval financing system," in Maloney's words — in a (largely successful) effort to evade electronic detection by international authorities. On the other, American and European officials employ computerized information sharing to investigate open source public records, electronically linked bank accounts, and so on in an effort to track and disrupt terrorist financing networks — networks that by definition cannot be tracked by these avowedly "high-tech" mechanisms because they depend on pens, paper, handshakes, and trust to remain functional in an official globalized world linked by electronic technologies. (As Senator Graham of Florida would caustically put it on the Senate floor during a separate debate, "Unless al-Qaida develops a policy of transferring money entirely by ATMs, the FBI's current investigatory methods are unlikely to be very effective.")

This is historical catachresis at its worst, a blatant and confused misuse of terminology that registers a broader cognitive dissonance in the face of a category-defeating enemy. In the case of terrorist use of *hawala*, I would insist, low-tech is high-tech — or better, *hawala*'s low-techness implies a knowledge of high-tech on the part of al Qaeda that is sophisticated, thorough, and ineradicably *modern*. The last thing it is, in other words, is "medieval." There has nevertheless been a willful insistence among government officials on the intrinsically medieval character of *hawala*. Several years after the above exchange, in testimony before a House International Relations subcommittee on the Middle East and Central Asia, Robert Baer, a former CIA case officer, reminded his audience

> that many people in Saudi Arabia and the rest of the Middle East consider they're at war with us, yet [are] trying to remain our allies in a very difficult time. Many of these societies have medieval banking systems, private banks, and accounting procedures which don't match our standards. And they in fact have ways to get around funding terrorism, funding jihad, supporting Hamas, supporting the Islamic jihad, supporting Hezbollah in Lebanon.

While it may be true that these "medieval banking systems" fail to "match our standards," on the part of al Qaeda, at least, this mismatch represents a strategic choice to evade these standards, not an unsuccessful effort at modernization that somehow fails to achieve them.

What unites all of the post-9/11 verbiage I've been discussing so far is its collective promotion of a fallacy of historical continuity. George W. Bush and Osama bin Laden use the word "crusade," and therefore the Crusades have some kind of material relevance to the matters at hand. *Hawala* happens to have originated in Near Eastern civilizations during the ninth or tenth century, and therefore it's a "medieval financing system." (European bankers began charging interest on loans in the twelfth century. Is your mortgage therefore also part of a "medieval financing system"?).

Islamist mass murderers promote through violence against civilians their own twisted interpretation of a sacred text that happens to have been written in the eighth century, and their thoroughly and calculatedly modern theology becomes universally legible as "medieval." (The period from which bin Laden and his predecessor Qutb derived much of their theological argument is technically the classical period of Islam; Thomas Friedman could just as easily have referred to the 9/11 attackers as "classicists"!)

It may appear poor strategy for a medievalist to be arguing against the direct relevance of the Middle Ages to the political crises of our own moment. Yet one of the most purely ideological effects of post-9/11 medievalism has been its tendency to permit those who exploit its patina of historical responsibility to avoid engagement with the full complexities of *recent* history. Let me explain this another way, for the point is crucial. In the wake of September 11, it was the mind of the cold warrior, *not* the mind of the crusader, that was determined to overlook and even suppress the involvement of Saudi Arabian royalty in the financing of al Qaeda. It was a modern, cold war "state of consciousness," not the state of consciousness of the medieval crusader, that was willing to permit Pakistan's burgeoning international market in fissible nuclear material to go entirely unsanctioned as part of a strategic bid for that country's alliance in the war against the Taliban. And in launching a calculated attack on an Iraqi dictator whose regime the United States had done everything it could to arm, support, and excuse for over a decade (Donald Rumsfeld's warm handshake with Saddam Hussein in 1984 comes to mind), George W. Bush's "predecessor," in Carroll's terms, was not a medieval pope, but his own father. It is not the mentality, but the *rhetoric* of the crusader that keeps our gaze pinned to the hypnotist's medievalizing coin: the specifically modern crusader, however, who constantly speaks in Manichaean absolutes yet consistently betrays his schooling in the diffuse moral relativisms of the twentieth century.

PART II:
The New Middle Ages

History is the only laboratory we have in which to test the consequences of thought.

—Étienne Gilson

Of Buddhas and Baghdad:
Two Middle Ages

The Congress finds that—

...(18) in 762 A.D., the city of Baghdad, founded under the rule of al-Mansur, the second caliph of the Abbasid dynasty, was the central commercial, cultural, philosophical, and intellectual capital of the world... and for a time the center of an empire that stretched from Central Asia to Spain;

(19) the city of Baghdad contains the Kadhimain mosque, the shrines of Abu Hanifa and Abd al-Qader al-Gailani, and many other medieval buildings, including other tombs, mosques, minarets, and the 13th century Mustansiriya University (an Islamic law school);

(20) located sixty miles north of Baghdad is the Abbasid city of Samarra, the home to the famous Great Mosque, as well as the Abu Dalaf mosque with a spiral minaret, and other important buildings dating from 800-1200 A.D.;

(21) in the modern city of Samarra, the tombs of the Tenth and Eleventh Caliphs, as well as the portal for the return of the Twelfth Caliph, are of great significance for a major segment of Shi'a Islam;

(22) the tombs of the Fourth Caliph Ali and his son Husayn are located in Najaf and Karbala (respectively), which are the two most holy cities of the Shiite branch of Islam;

(23) located in Iraq's third largest city, Mosul, are a Great Mosque, dating from the late 9th or early 10th century A.D., and nearby an ancient leaning brick minaret, that is all that is left of an Ommayad mosque dating from 640 A.D....

—*from the Iraq Cultural Heritage Protection Act (HR 3497), in the U.S. House of Representatives, November 17, 2003*

To scan the text of HR 3497, shorthanded by its congressional sponsors as "The Iraq Cultural Heritage Protection Act" and introduced in November 2003, is to hear a joke repeated in tones of tragedy, farce, and more than a little irony. Intended by its well-meaning sponsors to prevent the export and foreign sale of irreplaceable artifacts looted from Iraqi museums and monuments in the early weeks of the U.S. invasion, the bill reads in hindsight like a tactical guide for the Iraqi insurgency, which continues to exploit the archaeological and cultural status of medieval graveyards, minarets, mosques, and other such sites as both targets for attack as well as protective hideouts for themselves and depots for extensive caches of weapons. It is now a commonplace that the American planners of the Iraq War had failed to predict or prevent the devastation of the country's "cultural heritage" in the form of numerous artifacts, sculptures, and other items pillaged from museums after the initial U.S. invasion; but these regrettable artistic losses pale in comparison to the devastation of Iraq's premodern urban architecture, a much more visible embodiment of the same medieval heritage that Rumsfeld and the Pentagon were excoriated for leaving vulnerable to indigenous looters. Over the next two years, even as the Congress was actively considering legislation aimed at preventing theft from Iraqi archives, museums, and repositories, the sheer volume and force of American weaponry was leveling thousand-year-old buildings and neighborhoods in Iraqi cities with little or no self-consciousness in its relentless effort to quell the insurgency.

A cycle of abnegated destruction of Iraq's "medieval heritage" continued without abatement well into 2005. Almost a year to the day after the revised bill was introduced in the House (after which it was buried in the Ways and Means Committee with no further action taken), U.S. troops began an all-out assault on the Iraqi city of Fallujah, accompanied by reports of entire city blocks of ancient, winding streets succumbing to American artillery barrages and air strikes. The capital city, meanwhile, was transformed into a milieu of insurgent bombings and coalition artillery that, taken together, have destroyed innumerable buildings and parts of buildings dating from the

Middle Ages. "Baghdad itself is a major medieval site," Columbia University archaeologist Zainab Bahrani, a native Iraqi, remarked a few years ago. "The city is filled with buildings from the ninth to the fourteenth centuries."

This tension between the legislative preservation and the physical destruction of the Iraqi premodern stands in stark contrast to the degraded status of all things medieval in the immediate wake of the 2001 attacks. Before September 11, we must recall, the Taliban's collective guilt in the eyes of the international community derived chiefly from its strict iconoclasm, which resulted in the spectacular destruction of two massive second-century statues, the Bamiyan Buddhas, earlier that same year (a destruction choreographed for the global media by Taliban propagandists). The number of news stories and governmental proclamations registering the world's outrage at the regime's explosive toppling of these statues dwarfed the number devoted to the Taliban's predilection for staging rituals of torture and mass execution of fellow Afghanis in soccer stadiums. Yet when American attention turned to the Taliban and al Qaeda in the months following the September 11 attacks, the Afghani premodern suddenly assumed a new identity: less as archaeological remains than as human military objective. Before our eyes, the Taliban was transformed from a fundamentalist, primitive regime isolated from the world and nuttily destroying majestic artworks into a sophisticatedly post-national regime whose putative medievalism was now understood as inextricable from its will and ability to sponsor global terror.

Yet we need to understand the discursive compulsion toward the medieval after September 11 as more than just another chapter in the long history of medievalism as an idiom of essentialism, backwardness, alterity, primitivism, and so on. In part it surely is such a chapter, and I wouldn't want to deny the dehumanizing force of such representations of the attackers as a "band of medieval barbarians" in front of a congressional committee plotting war. We nevertheless make a grave error in mistaking this commonplace late-Orientalist species of medievalism for the strategic deployment of the premodern at the upper levels of the Bush administration — and in particular within the neoconservative elite that designed, implemented, and justified the wars in Afghanistan and Iraq. As I'll explain, it is here, in the fertile ground of neoconservative reflection and policy, that we most need to distinguish garden-variety medievalism from neomedievalism, and to understand the role of neomedievalism in the service of a long-standing preoccupation among neoconservatives with the transformation of the nature of international relations following the end of the Cold War.

The more paranoid part of me wants to see this forked-tongued medievalism as a deliberate and fully conscious strategy on the part of the communications apparatus of the departments of Defense and Justice. As Stanley Kubrick asked of *Dr. Strangelove*,

> After all, what could be more absurd than the very idea of two megapowers willing to wipe out all human life because of an accident, spiced up by political differences that will seem as meaningless to

Wolfie in the Middle

To demonstrate what I mean by this heuristic distinction between medievalism and neomedievalism, I want to pause over a series of public statements by two neoconservative figures formerly at the upper echelons of the Department of Defense. (For reasons that will become clear I will be quoting these figures at some length.) Currently the president of the World Bank, Paul D. Wolfowitz served as Deputy Secretary of Defense in the years following September 11. A consummate anti-realist, Wolfowitz represented in many ways the apotheosis of neoconservatism within the Bush administration, rendering the nearly obsessive medievalism subtending his speeches during the

War on Terror all the more provocative. Here I'll cite just a small selection of excerpts from Wolfowitz's public pronouncements over the calendar year following the September 11 attacks:

> We've said over and over again, correctly, this is not a war against the Afghan people, it's a war against foreign terrorists who have penetrated Afghanistan and a medieval sort of regime that is oppressing the people of Afghanistan.
>
> *Interview with* London Sunday Telegraph,
> *October 26, 2001*

> The attacks that came so suddenly and so brutally on a date that is now etched in our national consciousness were targeted not only against our citizens and our buildings — the attacks of September 11th were targeted against everything that defines America — targeted by oppressors who seek to impose on their own people an almost medieval regime of terror.
>
> *Remarks to the Fletcher Conference,*
> *Ronald Reagan Building and International Trade*
> *Center, Washington, DC, November 14, 2001*

> You know I lived in Indonesia for three years. I know what Indonesian Muslims are like, and their view of the religion is not at all this medieval view that the Taliban tried to impose on the Afghan people.
>
> *Interview with Indonesian Television,*
> *November 28, 2001*

> We need to recognize that the terrorists target not only us but their fellow Muslims, upon whom they

aim to impose a medieval, intolerant and tyrannical way of life.

Remarks to the World Affairs Council,
Monterey, CA, May 3, 2002

Terrorism is not something new to Asia. The Tokyo subway attack was one of them, should have been a wake-up call to the whole world and these terrorists, the ones that we're most concerned today have as their principal target the world's Muslim population. They want to take those billion Muslims and lock them up in a kind of a medieval darkness that will serve their ends.

Interview with Asahi Shimbun,
Singapore, May 31, 2002

We need to recognize that the terrorists target not only the West, but they also target their fellow Muslims, upon whom they would impose a medieval, intolerant and tyrannical way of life.

"The Gathering Storm: The Threat of Global Terror
and Asia/Pacific Security," Remarks to the
International Institute for Strategic Studies, Asia
Security Conference: The Shangri-La Dialogue,
Singapore, June 1, 2002

[I]t is important to keep repeating that these values that the terrorists target are not only Western values. They're universal values. That what the terrorists most aspire to do is to take the world's billion Muslims back to a twisted, medieval notion of what the proper order of things is. A world in which women are oppressed, in which religious bigotry and extremism are promoted, a world in which children are indoctrinated to hate is not, I believe, a world that most of the world's Muslims want to live in.

And we need to help them, and help ourselves, in fighting them.

Speech to the Hoover Institution,
Washington, DC, June 5, 2002

We find ourselves standing together, both our countries believing deeply in democracy, in human rights, both of our countries threatened by terrorists who deeply oppose those values and who believe in the killing of innocents as a way to advance their terrible agenda — which is an agenda that aims to take the world's Muslim population back to some medieval notion of intolerance and bigotry and repression.

Press Conference at Manila Peninsula Hotel,
June 30, 2002

Indonesia has 200 million Muslims, practice a very tolerant approach to religion and to religious matters and great respect for other religions in their country, but I think there is something of a struggle in the Muslim world between that point of view — the tolerant, open-minded point of view, which I think in their hearts is what most Muslims aspire to, and this extremist, almost medieval view that is represented by the Taliban and some of the more extreme regimes in the Middle East.

Interview with National Public Radio, July 2, 2002

I had the pleasure of experience in very tolerant Muslim majority societies. And that's, I believe, the real future for Muslims and some of the versions that you mentioned are not noticeably different from al Qaeda or the Taliban. And it seems to be the objective to oppose the kind of so-called medieval tyranny — but it was pointed out to me that were better; it's almost the twentieth century kind of totalitarian view of how people should be ruled by an ideology, in this case with a certain Muslim overtone.

Interview with Turkish Print Journalists,
July 17, 2002

I believe in the enormous value of democracy and I feel from the many Turks that I know that the belief in Turkey in tolerance and in secularism in some form, you can argue what that means, is so strong that I'm reasonably confident whatever happens in any individual election that the direction of Turkey in the long term is pretty clear, and that if anyone tries to impose a sort of medieval religious view on the Turkish people they're going to fail.

Interview with the Hurriyet *(Turkey),*
August 20, 2002

[W]hen I look at the people who did the terrible bombing in Bali and then killed more Indonesians in Jakarta and the people who killed Jews and Muslims and Christians in Istanbul and the people who killed people of all faiths in the World Trade Center, and you know what the list looks like. Their goal seems to be to take the Muslim world in particular back to a sort of medieval, fanatical view of life. And progress is their enemy and freedom is their enemy.

Press Availability, Washington, DC,
February 2, 2004

If this string of utterances from the second-in-command at the Defense Department seems unremarkable in its parts, the sheer number of Wolfowitz's public assessments of Islamist backwardness in these terms (and I've reproduced just a small fraction of such statements) renders the totality of his nearly obsessive medievalism somewhat astonishing. These are not unfortunate metaphors, as Bush's invocation of "crusade" likely was. In most cases they occur as part of comments scripted in advance by Wolfowitz himself and by the office of communications at the Department of Defense, an engine of neoconservative discourse in the Bush administration. In other words, the medievalism of al Qaeda and the Taliban became a calculated and consistent part of Pentagon agitprop during the first year of the War on Terror, a period in which every word coming from a senior administration official was parsed around the world for its implications for American foreign policy and military intentions. Wolfowitz's banal rhetoric of medievalism — imputing darkness, lack of women's rights, intolerance, oppression, fanaticism, brutality, terror, extremism, bigotry, and so on to the enemy's failure of modernity — goes hand in hand with the clash-of-civilizations neoconservatism that seeks to promote American exceptionalism as the guiding and forceful principle of state-centered global policy.

But consider Wolfowitz's historical imagination in relation to that of his then-boss, former Secretary of Defense Donald Rumsfeld, testifying before the Senate Appropriations Committee in support of the defense authorization bill in April of 2005. "To the seeming surprise of some," Rumsfeld said in his opening statement,

> our enemies have brains. They are constantly adapting and adjusting to what we're doing. They

combine medieval sensibilities with modern technology and media savvy to find new ways to exploit perceived weaknesses and to weaken the civilized world.

It would be easy to read Rumsfeld's language here as yet another iteration of the medievalism that Friedman et al. had imputed to the attackers back in 2001, particularly when taken in conjunction with Rumsfeld's closing comments that day:

> Mr. Chairman, across the world, brave men and women wearing America's uniform are doing the hard work of history. Bringing the hope of freedom to some of the darkest corners of the Earth will render a powerful blow to the forces of extremism who have killed thousands of innocent people in our country and across the globe.

The "hard work of history" is precisely to defeat the "medieval sensibilities" of the enemy, bringing the light of hope to those living in the darkness of barbarism.

Yet Rumsfeld is saying something fundamentally distinct from Wolfowitz and others, and it's this difference that begins to register the complexity of specifically neocon medievalism. Consider where these "medieval sensibilities" appear in this opening statement from his prepared remarks delivered that day:

> We are here today to discuss the President's Fiscal Year 2006 request for the Department as well as funding for ongoing operations in the Global War on Terror. Before discussing dollars, programs and weapons, let me offer some context for the tasks

ahead. When President Bush took office over four years ago, he recognized the need to transform America's defense establishment to meet the unconventional and unpredictable threats of the 21st Century. The attacks of September 11th gave new urgency and impetus to efforts then underway to make our Armed Forces a more agile, expeditionary and lethal force. The national security apparatus of the United States has undergone, and continues to undergo, historic changes on a number of fronts.

We have confronted and are meeting a variety of challenges:

- The urgency of moving military forces rapidly across the globe;
- The necessity of functioning as a truly joint force — as opposed to simply de-conflicting the Services;
- The need to recognize we are engaged in a war and yet still bound by a number of peacetime constraints, regulations and requirements, against an enemy unconstrained by laws; and
- Adjusting to a world where the threat is not from a single superpower, but from various regimes and extremist cells that can work together and proliferate lethal capabilities.

After more than three years of conflict, two central realities of this struggle are clear. First is that this struggle cannot be won by military means alone. The Defense Department must continue to work with other government agencies to successfully employ all instruments of national power. We can no longer think in terms of neat, clear walls between departments and agencies, or even committees of jurisdiction in Congress. The tasks ahead are far too complex to remain wedded to old divisions....

The Department continues to reevaluate our contingency plans, operations, and force structure in light of the technological advances of the past decade. ...In consultation with Congress and our allies, the Department is making long overdue changes in U.S. global basing, moving away from fixed Cold War garrisons and towards an ability to surge quickly to wherever capability is needed...

The Pentagon also began to change the way it does business. We have adopted an evolutionary approach to acquisition. Instead of waiting for an entire system to be ready before fielding it, this approach has made it possible, for example, to more rapidly field new robots to detonate roadside bombs in Iraq.

Some thoughts about the future. To the seeming surprise of some, our enemies have brains. They are constantly adapting and adjusting to what we're doing. They combine medieval sensibilities with modern technology and media savvy to find new ways to exploit perceived weaknesses and to weaken the civilized world.

We must employ the lessons of the past three and half years of war to be able to anticipate, adjust, act and react with greater agility. These necessary reforms have encountered, and will continue to encounter, resistance. It is always difficult to depart from the known and the comfortable. ...But, consider the challenge our country faces to not only reorganize the military, but to also transform the enormous Defense bureaucracy and fight two wars at the same time. And, if that were not enough, to do all this for the first time in an era with:

- 24 hour worldwide satellite news coverage, with live coverage of terrorist attacks, disasters and combat operations;

- Cell phones;
- Digital cameras;
- Global internet;
- E-mail;
- Embedded reporters;
- An increasingly casual regard for the protection of classified documents and information;
- and a U.S. government still organized for the Industrial Age, not the Information Age.

Mr. Chairman, the President's Fiscal Year 2006 Budget request makes some tough choices and proposes to fund a balanced combination of programs to develop and field the capabilities most needed by America's military.

Again, these are prepared remarks, written by Rumsfeld in conjunction with the Defense Department's Office of Communications, and one thing that's so striking here is how Rumsfeld's argument ascribes to the medievalism of the enemy its ability to adapt new technologies and medias to its designs. For Rumsfeld, the medievalism of al Qaeda is not religious fanaticism, or at least it is not most urgently that. Rather, our enemies combine medieval sensibilities with modern technology and media savvy to find new ways to exploit perceived weaknesses. The enemy's medievalism is inseparable from its character as an agile, adaptable, transnational, multimedia organization.

The "medieval sensibilities" of the enemy, then, are tactical, and they must be met with newly medieval sensibilities of our own. Our military must be more mobile, its communications infrastructure more adaptable and flexible, and we must operate in a theater characterized above all by the fluidity of national boundaries and jurisdictions (even the nods to other nations and their cooperation feels outdated here). "The tasks ahead," Rumsfeld avows, "are far too complex to remain wedded to old divisions."

An equally clear distillation of Rumsfeld's views on force innovation came more recently in the form of the Quadrennial Defense Review for 2006, a fascinating case study in neoconservative adaptation to new transnational realities. One of the sections near the end, entitled "Developing a 21st Century Total Force," recognizes the immensity of this evolutionary enterprise:

> The Department of Defense is the world's largest employer, directly employing more than three million people. The Department's Total Force — its active and reserve military components, its civil servants, and its contractors — constitutes its warfighting capability and capacity. Members of the Total Force serve in thousands of locations around the world, performing a vast array of duties to accomplish critical missions.

Despite its national mission, the Department of Defense has become nothing less than a transnational corporation in its own right, a new Ecclesia in its globe-spanning immensity. The Total Force as envisioned by Rumsfeld will allow for "routine integration with foreign and domestic counterparts," including the many NGOs with which it will network and cooperate. More disturbingly, perhaps, the "traditional and visible distinction between war and peace is less clear at the start of the 21st century," the Review insists. "In a long war, the United States expects to face large and small contingencies at unpredictable levels." Here, the Defense Department avows, is where the enemy's "medieval sensibilities" threaten to merge most seamlessly with their medievalist tactics, as they "target symbols of modernity like skyscrapers with civilian jetliners used as missiles." In short, "The Department's current structure and processes are handicaps in the protracted fight we now face against agile and networked foes": foes whose motivations for war and strategies for its execution merge into a single "medieval vision of the future," as Rumsfeld put it after the death of Abu Musab al-Zarqawi.

The New Medievalism

In his statement read in front of a Senate committee and in the Quadrennial Defense Review, Rumsfeld is speaking a particular language, a language that arises from a strand of scholarship in the field of International Relations that I believe is increasingly shaping the work of think tanks and the framing of government policy initatives in the wake of September 11. This subfield of International Relations theory is called *neomedievalism*, and it has its origins in the writings of the British political theorist Hedley Bull. An English-school realist, Bull was one of the first prominent theorists of International Relations to argue for the emerging challenge of non-state or post-state actors to a field that was overwhelmingly dominated by nation- and state-centered approaches. His much-cited book *The Anarchical Society: A Study of Order in World Politics*, first published in 1977 and now considered a realist classic of IR theory, outlined a series of "alternative paths to world order," among them "world government," a "disarmed world," the "solidarity of states" (involving the strengthening of the UN or a similar body), "ideological homogeneity" among existing states, and other possible scenarios. In the process, Bull outlined one particularly counterintuitive model for "the future structure of world politics that could replace the system of sovereign states":

> It is... conceivable that sovereign states might disappear and be replaced not by a world government but by a modern and secular equivalent of the kind of universal political organisation that existed in Western Christendom in the Middle Ages. In that system no ruler or state was sovereign in the sense of being supreme over a given territory and a given segment of the Christian population; each had to share authority with vassals beneath, and with the Pope and (in Germany and Italy) the Holy Roman Emperor above. The universal political order of Western Christendom represents an alternative to the system of states which does not yet embody universal government.
>
> All authority in mediaeval Christendom was thought to derive ultimately from God and the political system was basically Theocratic. It might therefore seem fanciful to contemplate a return to the mediaeval model, but it is not fanciful to imagine that there might develop a modern and secular

counterpart of it that embodies its central characteristic: a system of overlapping authority and multiple loyalty.

Though Bull devoted a mere page and a half to this "mediaeval model," he invested it with deep implications for the nature of political sovereignty in the modern world:

> if modern states were to come to share their authority over their citizens, and their ability to command their loyalties, on the one hand with regional and world authorities, and on the other hand with substate or sub-national authorities, to such an extent that the concept of sovereignty ceased to be applicable, then a neo-mediaeval form of universal political order might be said to have emerged.

The advantages of this neo-medieval form, according to Bull, would include a "structure of overlapping authorities and crisscrossing loyalties" that would avoid the danger of the states system while eluding the over-reach of world government. The disadvantages could well include "more ubiquitous and continuous violence and insecurity" than that existing under the modern states system. Again, while this initial formulation of neomedievalism by an IR theorist was short-winded, it typifies what subsequent work in this area has recognized as Bull's imaginative challenges to settled paradigms. As he put it in *The Anarchical Society*, "our view of possible alternatives to the states system should take into account the limitations of our own imagination and our own inability to transcend past experience."

Following Bull's proposal in the seventies of a premodern turn in world politics, neomedievalism (or "The New Medievalism," as others have dubbed it) grew into an influential school of thought within IR theory, particularly following the demise of the Cold War in the early nineties. As one proponent described it some years ago, what is shared among neomedievalist theorists of international relations is the recognition that

> sovereignty is becoming more fluid. States are increasingly required to share power and authority with subnational units (such as vassals of old), supernational political entities (likened to a Holy Roman Empire), and powerful nongovernmental forces (analogous to the Roman Catholic Church). Regional integration [serves] as a counterweight to state particularism. Technology [is] making state authority less and less relevant, even while private international violence is proliferating.

As the almost offhand rhetoric of homology here implies ("such as," "likened to," "analogous to"), the neomedievalists make few claims to the historical veracity of the Middle Ages they propose as a model for the current state of international relations, and it may seem wrong-headed to take them to task for historical misrepresentation when what they're proffering is, in effect, a compelling heuristic model of post-national world politics. A key part of neomedievalism can be found in the *neo*: these theorists are arguing not for the simple return of an archaic model of non-state action, but for the emergence of something fundamentally new that might helpfully be understood by historical analogy. Neil Winn, one of the most thoughtful of these theorists, observes that the "neo-medievalist metaphor... takes a wider, if looser, view" of the current state of international affairs than that found in competing state-centered analyses, "highlighting a series of broad yet fundamental 'challenges' which the modern international state system currently faces." Its acknowledged critical flexibility as metaphor has allowed neomedievalism to emerge as a remarkably cogent framework for analyzing contemporary nonstate actors, and it is now common to find sections of IR textbooks and guidebooks devoted to the neomedievalist school.

I think it important to recognize in this respect the argumentative distinction between IR neomedievalism theory and the "Three Worlds" model of globalization propagated in so-called modernization theory (including such works as Strayer's *On the Medieval Origins of the Modern State* with which I began). Even in Talcott Parson's *The System of Modern Societies*, to take a particularly influential example, we only rarely see the Middle Ages functioning as a fallow background to the emergence of modern polity and statecraft. As Parson puts it,

> The very considerable period of uneven development and transition between the end of the Middle Ages and the first crystallization of modern society largely resulted from the subtle combination in medieval society of features favoring modernization and features, basically incompatible with modernity, that could become foci of resistance to modernization.

Here Parsons is forthrightly proposing the medieval as the institutional and ideological crucible of modernity: an engine of dialectical modernization that would ultimately result in the formation of the states system in the West.

Immediately following the attacks of September 11, however, it was not the rehashed assumptions of Cold War modernization theory that served to explain the new enemy's alleged medievalism. Rather it was neomedievalism, this purely academic analogy, this highly allegorical and counterintuitive theory of how the world looks in the decade following the collapse of the Soviet Union, that would explode into currency in think tank discourse and within policy-making bodies in the Departments of Defense and State and the newly-founded Department of Homeland Security. P.R. Singer's studies on post-state militarism, particularly his book *Corporate Warriors*, a bestseller in military-industrial think tanks over the last two years, envisions feudal analogies derived from his understanding of medieval mercenary culture as the most compelling historical model for the corporatization of sub- and cross-national warfare in recent decades. In an interview following the publication of the book, Singer explicitly identifies the "trend ...to what people have called neo-Medievalism" as the underlying thrust of his own thesis:

> You have a system developing that has, much like the Middle Ages, multiple actors, both sovereign and not, and all of them contending within the system. Some of them will have legitimacy but not power, such as the UN. Others will have power, but not

legitimacy, like drug cartels, terrorist groups. A question mark is where private military contractors will fall into this. You'll have states, both powerful and states in name only. So you have basically this massive system, which is a lot more complex and difficult than the very simple view of the balance of power that we saw in the state sovereign system.

There have also been a number of timely collections such as *Neomedievalism and Civil Wars*, a book that went into production soon after September 11 and includes several chapters on terrorism and neomedievalism that read in retrospect like virtual scripts of the prologue and aftermath of the attacks.

Neomedievalism reached its apogee of accessibility, in fact, just as I was completing the first draft of this book. In the May-June 2006 issue of *Foreign Affairs* appears an essay by John Rapley titled "The New Middle Ages." (*Foreign Affairs*, it hardly needs to be said, is the most influential journal of international relations published in English, including among its avid readers Bill Clinton and Condoleeza Rice.) The abstract appearing at the head of the article captures in two sentences the global trend Rapley is diagnosing:

> The Middle Ages ended when the rise of capitalism on a national scale led to powerful states with sovereignty over particular territories and populations. Now that capitalism is operating globally, those states are eroding and a new medievalism is emerging, marked by multiple and overlapping sovereignties and identities — particularly in the developing world, where states were never strong in the first place.

Though the article features some wince-making sentences ("What killed off the European Middle Ages was capitalism"), it signals what I think we can safely call the mainstreaming of neomedievalism: its sudden, post-9/11 transformation from provocative academic theory into an idiom of global transformation far-reaching in its implications for America's own understanding of new forms of non-state hegemony and transnational sovereignty.

A measure of the recent institutional influence of this school of thought can be found in a forceful advocation of neomedievalism by a prominent IR theorist in an essay significant not for the originality of its argument in relation to previous work in the field, but for the context of its publication. The article appears in a recent volume of the *Naval War College Review*, which is required reading in the policy and planning wings of the Defense Department. As this theorist writes here,

> [T]errorism is merely one dimension of a wider phenomenon that is transforming the international system and domestic politics too around the world — neomedievalism, a phenomenon that is leading to the emergence of a new security dilemma in world politics... broadly speaking, neomedievalism means that we are increasingly in the presence of a plurality of overlapping, competing, and intersecting power structures — institutions, political processes, economic developments, and social transformations — above, below, and cutting across states and the states system. States today represent only one level of this power structure, becoming more diffuse, internally split, and enmeshed in wider

complex webs of power. This structure is fluid and fungible, feeding back and undergoing continual adjustments and ad hoc responses to a rapidly changing environment. In this context, the definition of what is a "security" issue is also becoming more and more fluid and fungible — including the dislocations caused by economic development; the destabilizing effect of transitions to democracy; the undermining of traditional cultures, beliefs, and loyalties; threats to the environmental and public health; and the like.

The resemblance here to Rumsfeld's innovatory rhetoric in regard to armed forces restructuring is anything but coincidental. For despite neomedievalism's origins within a strongly realist strain of international law and relations, it has infused neoconservative policy in the years since September 11 in a variety of ways and from a number of institutional viewpoints. Thus Deepak Lal, in an address to the American Enterprise Institute, a bastion of neoconservative ideology whose influence on administration policy-making would be difficult to exaggerate, writes of the nature of post-9/11 legality:

> Crucial in understanding this extension of the international rule of law is that it covered what was previously Christendom in Europe and in the new world, and the role of the medieval Catholic Church in providing the first "international" legal system.

Lal's sense of the new world order makes a strong historical claim derived directly from IR neomedievalism: that the Catholic Church provides an initial model of transnational law, and that international relations

post-9/11 must understand its analogical rootedness
in the premodern world if it hopes to address responsibly the contemporary nature of international legal relations. During the Iraq War, too, neomedievalism has
functioned as a kind of diagnostic for predicting the
fragmentation of the post-Saddam nation. Thus Jeremy
Greenstock, the UK's former envoy to Iraq, remarks in
an interview,

> There's never going to be a Western-style democ-
> racy in Iraq. The worst-case scenario is an implosion
> of Iraqi security and society down to levels lower
> than a nation-state, perhaps back to the medieval
> picture of local baronies.

So why does all of this matter? One of the
tenets of progressive critiques of neoconservatism has
been an abiding confidence in the näiveté of neoconservatives in the face of an increasing global complexity
following the Cold War. Unlike the realists, this
assumption tells us, the neocons don't understand the
transformative nature of transnationalism and the
power of the non-state actor, both of which they
subordinate to a belief in a community of sovereign
nation-states guided by the democratizing principles
and military superiority of an American Empire — a
belief wedded to an enduring distrust of international
institutions. "The state is their god," one prominent
critic of neoconservatism has written, "and they derive
their power from extending its reach." This is the critical thrust of Michael Hardt and Antonio Negri's
Empire, which seeks to dislodge the very concept of
empire from its origins in national formations (and it is

notable that Augustinian theology and Franciscan and Dominican mendicancy play a central role in Hardt and Negri's exposition). While this critique is certainly valid for the pre- and immediately post-9/11 context, for me the most compelling aspect of neoconservative neomedievalism is how it suggests that the neocons may finally be getting it — and not only getting it, but recruiting it, exploiting it, and using it to their own tactical advantage as they adapt their juridical and diplomatic languages to the full complexities of the post-9/11 world.

In its current form, neomedievalism is above all a paradigm for neoconservative intellectual renewal.

Neomedievalism
and the Torture Memos

In this spirit, the last part of this book addresses what I have found to be the most concrete and chilling instance of neomedievalism as it has functioned on the level of policy during the War on Terror. In January of 2002, over two years before the Abu Ghraib story broke, senior officials in the Bush administration initiated a series of upper-level conversations regarding the decision recently reached by the Department of Justice that the 1949 Geneva Convention III Relative to the Treatment of Prisoners of War (which I will hereafter shorthand as GPW) did not apply to prisoners taken by U.S. forces during the war in Afghanistan against al Qaeda and the Taliban. Preserved in a set of extraordinary memoranda between officials at Justice, the Department of State, the Department of Defense, and the White House, this debate among executive branch officials became widely known only in the wake of Abu Ghraib, when various press leaks, Freedom of Information Act requests, and commissioned investigations thrust these previously confidential exchanges into the public eye. The "torture papers," now readily available in a number of anthologies organized around the issue of America's promotion and practice of torture during the War on Terror, have been received with a steady mixture of horror from foreign and domestic human rights activists; righteous defensiveness and moral relativism from American politicians on both the right and the left; and bland inevitability from much of the American political class. Most of the criticism of these documents has focused, quite rightly, on their end result: the gruesome and humiliating torture and even murder of detainees at the hands of American military and intelligence personnel and the failure of the administration to respond with any honesty or accountability.

Despite the reams of published and on-line commentary devoted to these now notorious documents, however, there have been surprisingly few critiques of the particular logic of justification leading up to this conclusion beyond the general consensus that the Bush administration deemed it expedient in the pursuit of the war to torture detainees, and that it would do anything it could to find legal justification for doing so. White House counsel Alberto Gonzales's assessment of the Geneva Conventions' provisions on the treatment of detainees as "quaint" has thus become emblematic of the administration's supposedly cursory treatment of the question of justification. As in the case of Iraq's putative weapons of mass destruction, the Bush administration knew in advance what "facts" it wanted to uncover, and it channeled its legal queries, procedures, and findings accordingly. This was clearly the case for some of the central questions raised in the memos, for example, the issue of how to negotiate Article 5 of GPW:

> Should any doubt arise as to whether persons, having committed a belligerent act and having fallen into the hands of the enemy, belong to any of the categories enumerated in Article 4, such persons shall enjoy the protection of the present Convention until such time as their status has been determined by a competent tribunal.

Assistant Attorney General Jay S. Bybee, in a memorandum to Alberto Gonzales dated February 7, 2002, eliminated the tribunal problem by fiat: "A presidential determination ...would eliminate any legal 'doubt' as to the prisoners' status, as a matter of domestic law, and would therefore obviate the need for Article 5 tribunals." By this circular reasoning, if the president had decided there were no doubt as to the status of a particular detainee, then no doubt would there be.

While I would hardly want to dispute the more jaundiced assessments of the Bush administration's tactics, I do think they have tended to preempt a more in-depth analysis of the particular and often intricate logic undergirding its approach to specific questions of law raised in the memos, and this is true even for the considerable legal scholarship emerging in response to the documents. Perhaps the most pressing of these questions concerned the status of Taliban and al Qaeda forces under article 4 of GPW, which sought to define, in Bybee's words, "the types of persons who, once they have fallen under the control of the enemy, are entitled to the legal status of POWs." The importance of this initial determination cannot be overemphasized. If detainees *had* been designated "the types of persons" who deserved protection under GPW, the subsequent series of memos on the bounds of permissible interrogation would never have been written, and any incidents of abuse at Abu Ghraib and Guantánamo might well have been seen for what the administration continues to claim they were: isolated instances of misbehavior by individual U.S. troops acting against policy and violating orders. Before the administration and the military could decide how to stretch the definition of permissible interrogation techniques and avoid the charge of torture, in other words, their lawyers had to decide whether the present and future detainees in question would be granted "the legal status of POWs."

What makes these exchanges so remarkable is their promotion of an inexorable historical argument that might well have been scripted by neomedievalist IR theorists — as indeed on some level it was. The most widely cited of these papers was composed by Gonzales, then counsel to the President and, as of

February 2005, Attorney General of the United States. In a draft memorandum for Bush dated January 25, 2002, Gonzales sought to clarify some of the central "ramifications" of the president's apparent decision a week earlier that GPW did not apply to the conflict in Afghanistan. The overall aim of this infamous memorandum (which described the provisions of GPW as "obsolete") was to preempt a counterresponse from Secretary of State Colin Powell, who was arguing strongly (and, it turned out, belatedly) against the suspension of GPW for the Afghanistan conflict. Early on in the memo, Gonzales reiterates the two bases for the president's prior determination that GPW did not apply:

> As I discussed with you, the grounds for such a determination may include:
> - A determination that Afghanistan was a failed state because the Taliban did not exercise full control over the territory and people, was not recognized by the international community, and was not capable of fulfilling its international obligations (e.g., was in widespread material breach of its international obligations).
> - A determination that the Taliban and its forces were, in fact, not a government, but a militant, terrorist-like group.

What exactly a "terrorist-like" group as opposed to a terrorist group might be is not made explicit in the memo, though it is clear that Gonzales is projecting future legal strategy in what it calls "a new kind of war" with a new kind of enemy: "By concluding that GPW does not apply to al Qaeda and the Taliban,"

Gonzales writes, "we avoid foreclosing options for the future, particularly against nonstate actors."

Apparently unaware that the president's mind was already made up, Powell submitted a memo the next day that argued strongly for the continuing applicability of GPW standards to Taliban detainees. Once again, the status of Afghanistan as a coherent nation is at issue as Powell identifies the glaring inconsistency in Gonzales' argument:

> The Memorandum should note that any determination that Afghanistan is a failed state would be contrary to the official U.S. government position. The United States and the international community have consistently held Afghanistan to its treaty obligations and identified it as a party to the Geneva Conventions.

For Powell, Afghanistan, despite the corruption of its Taliban leadership, nevertheless is a nation, and the legal status of its armed forces should be managed accordingly. Indeed, as Powell notes, UN Security Council Resolution 1193 (passed by the Security Council with an affirmative vote from the United States in 1998) had stated unambiguously "its strong commitment to the sovereignty, independence, territorial integrity and national unity of Afghanistan, and its respect for its cultural and historical heritage" — and this was two years after the Taliban assumed power. This didn't deter Attorney General John Ashcroft from weighing in counterfactually in a memorandum dated February 1: "During relevant times of the combat, Afghanistan was a failed state. As such it was not a party to the treaty, and the treaty's protections do not apply."

All of this seems predictable enough. If you declare the nation you're fighting against as a non-nation, a "failed state," you change the very ontological nature of your enemy: you define the enemy down so it can be met on the battlefield without the headache of human rights and international law. Yet the particular intellectual justification behind this defining down is quite specific, and it figures most explicitly in one of the more complex memoranda, dated February 7, 2002 — the very date of the final and definitive directive from President Bush saying that the Geneva Conventions will not apply to the conflict. This memo comes from Jay S. Bybee, and it is directed to Alberto Gonzales:

> First, there is no organized command structure whereby members of the Taliban militia report to a military commander who takes responsibility for the actions of his subordinates. The Taliban lacks a permanent, centralized communications infrastructure. Periodically, individuals declared themselves to be "commanders" and organized groups of armed men, but these "commanders" were more akin to feudal lords than military officers. According to DoD, the Taliban militia functioned more as many different armed groups that fought for their own tribal, local, or personal interests.
>
> Moreover, when the armed groups organized, the core of the organization was often al Qaeda, a multinational terrorist organization, whose existence was not in any way accountable to or dependent upon the sovereign state of Afghanistan. We have previously concluded, as a matter of law, that al

Qaeda members are not covered by GPW.... After October 7, when the United States armed forces began aerial bombing of al Qaeda and Taliban targets in Afghanistan, the distinction between Taliban and al Qaeda became even more blurred as al Qaeda assumed the lead in organizing the defense.

The argument here is, I think, twisted and self-contradictory but brilliantly precise in its cynicism. Before the U.S. invasion of Afghanistan, Taliban commanders were tribal and decentralized, operating on a purely subnational, local level within Afghanistan. When these commanders and their local bands of warriors *did* organize, however, they did so through the mechanism of al Qaeda, whose multinational apparatus exceeded the sovereign bounds of the Afghan state — a sovereign state which, the other memos in the series argued, did not exist in the first place. Thus a constellation of local, sub-state sovereignties achieves coherence as a fighting force only once it is organized by a supra-national or transnational terrorist organization. "The sovereign state of Afghanistan" exists only as the measure of its failure. The key word in these paragraphs, obviously, is "feudal": *"these 'commanders' were more akin to feudal lords than military officers"* — feudal lords, however, whose ties of homage and military obligations have been recruited into the service of transnational networks of global terror.

And it is in that very dialectic between subnational feudal formations working for their own interests and transnational organizations working against and across national boundaries that we can most clearly see the impact of neomedievalist IR theory on the torture papers. In this respect, the specific chronology of the torture memos is crucial to an understanding of the administration's overall strategy in regard to GPW. The Gonzales-Powell exchanges, which became the most visible part of the administration's debate, came only after a condensed process of legal decision-making over the preceeding weeks embodied in several lengthier memoranda from administration lawyers. The most successful of these, dated January 9, 2002, was written jointly by John Yoo, Deputy Assistant Attorney General, and Robert J. Delahunty, Special Counsel to the Department of Justice.

One of the memo's central purposes was to establish clear criteria for determining the nature of a "failed state." "Afghanistan's status as a failed state is ground alone," Yoo-Delahunty suggest, "to find that members of the Taliban militia are not entitled to enemy POW status under the Geneva Convetions." More than this, they contend, "it appears from the public evidence that the Taliban militia may have been so intertwined with al Qaeda as to be functionally indistinguishable from it." Once again Taliban-controlled Afghanistan is both less than and more than a nation-state: a sub-national "militia" "intertwined" with the transnational Borg of al Qaeda. One of the first points of the memo's contestation of the GPW provisions concerns Article 3, which Yoo-Delahunty claim applies only to "large-scale conflicts bewteen a State and an insurgent group." What Yoo-Delahunty seek to exclude from coverage under GPW 3, in their own words, is

> a conflict between a State and a transnational terrorist group, which might operate from different terri-

torial bases, some of which might be located in
States that are parties to the Conventions and some
of which might not be. In such a case, the
Conventions would apply to a single armed conflict
in some scenes of action but not in others-which
seem inexplicable.

Inexplicable not just in practical terms, the memo
argues, but also historically vis-à-vis what Yoo-
Delahunty call "the distinct phases in the development
of the laws of war" postulated by International
Relations theorists. While traditional IR models had
relied on the model of the nation-state, the current and
new phase, Yoo-Delahunty contend, represents a
"complete break...with the traditional 'State-sover-
eignty-oriented approach' of international law." Article
3 of the Geneva Conventions, they argue, "was
prepared during a period in which the traditional,
State-centered view of international law was still dominant." Therefore, it is

> overwhelmingly likely that an armed conflict
> between a Nation State and a transnational terrorist
> organization, or between a Nation State and a failed
> State harboring and supporting a transnational
> terrorist organization, could not have been within
> the contemplation of the drafters of common
> Article 3.

Thus, when Yoo-Delahunty eventually come
around to the application of GPW and the US's own
War Crimes Act (WCA) to al Qaeda detainees, the writ-
ers can state definitively that "*Al Qaeda's status as a
non-state actor renders it ineligible to claim the protec-*

tions of the treatises specified by the WCA" (italics in the original). Al Qaeda, they avow, is "a non-governmental terrorist organization composed of members from many nations, with ongoing operations in dozens of nations." Yoo-Delahunty admit that the question of whether GPW3 applies to Taliban detainees "presents a more difficult legal question" than for al Qaeda, though the same logic would ultimately apply:

> The weight of informed opinion strongly supports the conclusion that, for the period in question, Afghanistan was a "failed state" whose territory had been largely overrun and held by violence by a militia or faction rather than by a government. Accordingly, Afghanistan was without the attributes of statehood necessary to continue as a party to the Geneva Conventions, and the Taliban militia, like al Qaeda, is therefore not entitled to the protections of the Geneva Conventions. Furthermore, there appears to be substantial evidence that the Taliban was so dominated by al Qaeda and so complicit in its actions and purposes that the Taliban leadership cannot be distinguished from al Qaeda, and accordingly that the Taliban milita cannot stand on a higher footing under the Geneva Conventions.

Already when this memo was written, in early January of 2002, the argument was essentially over. And the smoking gun? When Yoo-Delahunty back up their assertion about Afghanistan's status as a "failed state" with legal analysis from the field of International Relations, the first piece of scholarship they cite is an essay by Daniel Thurer published in 1999 in the *International Review of the Red Cross*. The essay concerns the status of the failed state in relation to international law and is devoted in large part to ways of redressing or correcting these failed states. As Thurer writes, future corrective efforts in this regard by coherent nation-states must be directed at overcoming "the old feudal system":

> The apparatus established by newly stabilized States for the exercise of authority must be gradually extended in order to provide an effective system of public services. To promote the welfare of the people, this system will also permit the resumption of relations formerly maintained with international development and social work organizations.

The nation-state, Thurer avows, must be at all costs the primary bulwark against the incursion of neomedievalism, which threatens to undermine state sovereignty in favor of a premodern barbarism and diffusion:

> Though its fragility is regularly revealed, the State based on the rule of law, thanks to the force of effective authority and the legitimacy thereof, has largely been able to control the destructive instincts of some sections of mankind and to provide support for the blossoming of the constructive "instinct of life." As far as civilization is concerned, its contribution, together with that of international law, has been to bring about objective systems of order separated and distanced from group identities. Our own modern State system has emerged out of the many different sources of power of the mediaeval empire. However, the age which now stands before us will be marked by a steady waning of the old sovereign

State and could lead to a new proliferation and fragmentation of socio-political forces. Thus, one of the
main challenges will be to transpose the achieve-
ments of the constitutional state system to the international level, so that mankind is saved from sliding
back into the barbarity of the past and that today's
"failed States" remain an isolated phenomenon.

This is the central neomedievalist realization, dressed
up here in its apocalyptic guise: that nations are in
decline, that the sovereign state threatens to be
submerged by "group identities" and fragmented
sovereignties embodied in the "barbarity of the past."
Failed states, that is to say, are medieval states, and they
must be overcome if modernity is to maintain its coherence as an international rather than transnational global
formation.

The argumentative logic that won the debate
within the Bush administration staged throughout the
torture memos, then, was in spirit and in letter a logic
of neomedievalism. Barbarity is backwardness and
primitivism, but it is also a contemporary incarnation
of "the many different sources of power of the maedi-
aeval empire." In this sense, the "medieval" in neomedievalism matters not a whit. It's the futurity, the
contemporaneity of this transnational medieval enemy
that renders it lethal — and that provides the Bush
administration in turn with the tactical means to defeat
it. As the memos make clear, the Bush administration
worked diligently to group "illegal combatants"
together as isolated bands of medieval warlords, affili-
ating its enemy with those very post-national "barbarians" apostrophized by Hardt and Negri in *Empire*. In

this sense, the torture memos embody a wider crisis over the terms of individual and collective identity in the War on Terror: a crisis in which those who lead a modern world of coherent nations, identifiable states, and established laws arrogate to themselves sovereignty over the inhabitants of a premodern milieu of multiple jurisdictions and scattered hegemonies that represent both its greatest tactical strength and its juridical Achilles' heel.

The Perils of "Traveling Theory"

The Torture Papers, then, confront us with an uncomfortable truth about post-9/11 medievalism. While Bush, Rumsfeld, Wolfowitz, and numerous others were busily choreographing medieval regimes, savage barbarians, and new crusades in their efforts to gear the nation for war, their lawyers and policy wonks were playing a parallel, elusive, but ultimately complementary medievalizing game of their own. This is why I believe it is so crucial to distinguish between that more familiar, "othering" kind of medievalist jargon favored by administration figures and mainstream and left journalists alike and the particular intellectual mechanism of neomedievalism within neoconservative discourse after

September 11. It's so much easier to expose and argue against the first kind. Whatever their actual military affiliations, most would agree, the detainees housed at Abu Ghraib and Guantánamo are individual human beings, entitled to human rights and legal representation, rather than a band of feudal warlords cut off from post-Enlightenment modernity. Some of them may indeed be aspiring mass murderers guided by a strand of classical Islamic theology, but they're not "medieval" aspiring mass murderers any more than Elizabeth II is a "medieval" queen because the English throne was once occupied by Richard II. This, I am afraid, is not a particularly challenging critique to articulate.

The effects of neomedievalism, on the other hand, the second subspecies of the neoconservative ideology of history, seem to me much more difficult to counter, even to discern, in part due to the marked disjunction between the theory's benign and gradual institutional emergence and its sudden and malicious appropriation by the neoconservatives over the last several years. For at heart, neomedievalism is a creation of the modern, Cold War and post-Cold War university. As such, its fate during the War on Terror gives us a frightening lens on to the ultimate co-optability of academic theorizing into a regressive and destructive political culture.

To put it another way, consider the commonality, both rhetorical and analytical, between International Relations theories of neomedievalism and the cluster of theoretical models prevalent within the humanities disciplines in recent decades. I'm generalizing irresponsibly here, but it's worth pointing out the extent to which neomedievalism's idiom of porous borders, overlapping authorities, conflicting jurisdictions, and so on can often be hard to distinguish from the postmodern-postcolonial patois those of us in literary studies have been speaking to one another over the last twenty years. Neomedievalism exhibits "a plurality of overlapping, competing, and intersecting power structures," as the *Foreign Affairs* article discussed above describes it: a phrase that could just as easily be lifted out of Foucault's *Discipline and Punish* — or, for that matter, a mediocre graduate essay in a postcolonial studies seminar. "The concept of Empire is characterized fundamentally by a lack of boundaries," Michael Hardt and Antonio Negri write in their year 2000 academic bestseller *Empire*. It is no accident that *Empire*, the ideal pre-9/11 academic distillation of postmodern "counter-globalization," derives much of its theoretical energy from the fluid categories it imports from a New Middle Ages it envisions as the very condition of *Empire*: the "nomad," the "new barbarians," the "lightness and joy" of St. Francis of Assisi that promise the enduring bliss of eternal resistance. *"Once again in postmodernity we find ourselves in Francis's situation,"* Hardt and Negri write (the italics are theirs), *"posing against the misery of power the joy of being."* Nor is it an accident that, after 9/11, the book's conservative critics hysterically decried *Empire* as a postmodern prophecy of left-wing moral relativism that lent ideological support to the suicide attackers themselves.

Indeterminacy, unknowability, deferral and *différance*, the fluidity of sovereignty, the border-transgressing promise of the transnational: we have laid claim to these tropes as our own critical stock in trade. It is no small measure of the shock accompanying the recent proliferation of neomedievalism that neoconservatism has begun to recruit these same tropes for its own continuing process of reinvention. To hear Donald Rumsfeld speaking this pomo idiom in the Quadrennial Defense Review; to see John Yoo in a memo to the Attorney General footnoting IR theories of neomedievalism; and thus to recognize that neomedievalism has devolved from intellectual paradigm to implicit justification of torture — these should serve as chilling reminders that, as Edward Said recognized, theory travels, and that those involved in any theory's institutional emergence and consolidation may end up having little or no say over the ethics of its extra-institutional deployment.

Neomedievalism began as a metaphor, an extended theoretical analogy. It was a creative way of imagining the global present and future by measuring its trends and tendencies against those characterizing a professedly schematic vision of the Middle Ages. Yet virtually every criterion of neomedievalist IR theory concerning the disintegration of states, the waning of national sovereignty, and the resultant transformations in the character of international law and diplomacy figures in the torture memos as a justification for the negation of human rights. The non-state actor here functions as a paradoxically close ally to this "state of exception," in Giorgio Agamben's phrase; non-statism writ large becomes the brute, premodern condition, the very justification of U.S. exceptionalism in defiance of the Geneva Conventions. If, as Thomas Friedman

Also available from Prickly Paradigm Press:

continued